THE LITTLE BOOK OF
GRANDMOTHER'S LOVE

First published in 2025 by OH
An Imprint of HEADLINE PUBLISHING GROUP LIMITED

1

Cataloguing in Publication Data is available from the British Library

ISBN 978-1-03542-282-1

Compiled and written by: Victoria Denne
Editorial: Saneaah Muhammad
Designed and typeset in Joanna Nova by: Tony Seddon
Project manager: Russell Porter
Production: Arlene Lestrade
Printed and bound in Dubai

Headline's policy is to use papers that are natural, renewable and recyclable products and made from wood grown in well-managed forests and other controlled sources. The logging and manufacturing processes are expected to conform to the environmental regulations of the country of origin.

HEADLINE PUBLISHING GROUP LIMITED
An Hachette UK Company
Carmelite House, 50 Victoria Embankment, London EC4Y 0DZ

The authorised representative in the EEA is Hachette Ireland, 8 Castlecourt Centre, Castleknock Road, Castleknock, Dublin 15, D15 YF6A, Ireland

www.headline.co.uk   www.hachette.co.uk

THE LITTLE BOOK OF
GRANDMOTHER'S LOVE

TIMELESS WISDOM AND WARMTH

CONTENTS

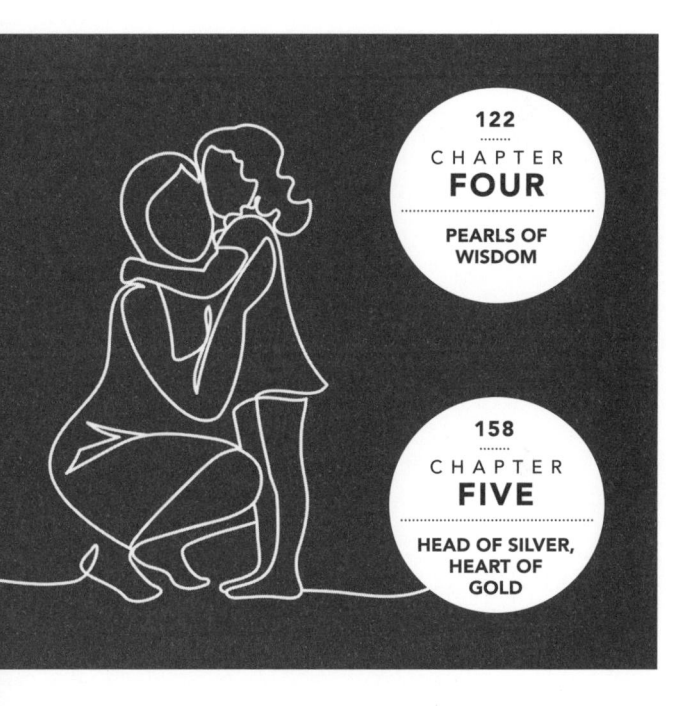

INTRODUCTION

Welcome, dear reader, to a treasury of warmth, wisdom and womanhood, in celebration of the incomparable love of grandmothers.

As we all know, grandmothers are a unique breed. They possess a magical ability to soothe the most turbulent tempers with a single hug and transform a mundane afternoon into an epic adventure with tales of their youth. They're the keepers of family secrets, the makers of the best pies, and the champions of spoiling us rotten – all while teaching us the most important life lessons. Grandmothers aren't just part of the family; they're the glue that holds it all together, with a cheeky smile and freshly baked goods.

In these pages, you will discover pearls of wisdom, snippets of humour and heartwarming affirmations that capture the essence of a grandmother's love. Ranging from the hilariously candid to the profoundly touching, these words serve as a testament to the irreplaceable role these women play in our lives, and the enduring and often magical bond between grandmothers and their grandchildren. Whether you're flipping through these pages to reminisce about the beloved grandmother in your life, or reflecting on your own transformation into one, we've got you covered.

So, settle into your favourite reading nook, perhaps with a cup of tea (just as your nan would have it), and let yourself be enveloped in the warm embrace of a grandmother's love.

CHAPTER 1

Nana Love

Just like most grandmas,
we're not going to beat around
the bush.

So, let's dive straight in
and discover what makes the role
of grandmother such a unique
one – especially to the
grandchildren she loves (and
spoils) so wholeheartedly…

66

Every parent knows that children look at their grandparents as sources of wisdom and security.

99

David Jeremiah

66

A child needs a grandparent, anybody's grandparent, to grow a little more securely into an unfamiliar world.

99

Charles and Ann Morse

66

Parent–child relationships
are complex. Grandmother–
grandchild relationships are
simple. Grandmas are short on
criticism and long on love.

99

Janet Lanese

66

Grandmothers always
have time to talk and
make you feel special.

99

Catherine Pulsifer

66

A grandmother pretends
she doesn't know who
you are on Halloween.

99

Erma Bombeck

66

Every house needs a
grandmother in it.

99

Louisa May Alcott

> **"**
> The simplest toy, one which even the youngest child can operate, is called a grandparent.
> **"**

Sam Levenson

"

A grandam's name
is little less in love
than is the doting
title of a mother.

"

William Shakespeare

66

Grandparents, like
heroes, are as necessary
to a child's growth
as vitamins.

99

Joyce Allston

"

A grandmother is a little bit parent, a little bit teacher, and a little bit best friend.

"

Unknown

66

A grandma is warm hugs and sweet memories. She remembers all of your accomplishments and forgets all of your mistakes.

99

Barbara Cage

"

Grandmothers are voices
of the past and role
models of the present.
Grandmothers open the
doors to the future.

"

Helen Ketchum

66

Grandmother's and roses are much the same. Each is a God's masterpiece with different names.

99

Unknown

66

A grandmother is
someone with silver
in her hair and gold
in her heart.

99

Unknown

66

Some of the world's
best educators are
grandparents.

99

Charles W. Shedd

66

A grandma is someone
who's dear in every way.
Her smile is like the
sunshine that brightens
each new day.

99

Unknown

66

Grandmother, the true power behind the power.

99

Lisa Birnbach

66
A grandmother is
a safe haven.
99

Suzette Haden Elgin

66

If you would civilize a man, begin with his grandmother.

99

Victor Hugo

66

A grandmother is
a babysitter who watches
the kids instead of
the television.

99

Unknown

66

Grandparents should play the
same role in the family as an elder
statesman can in the government of
a country. They have the experience
and knowledge that comes from
surviving a great many years of life's
battles and the wisdom, hopefully,
to recognize how their grandchildren
can benefit from this.

99

Geoff Dench

66

Uncles and aunts, and cousins,
are all very well, and fathers and
mothers are not to be despised;
but a grandmother, at holiday
time, is worth them all.

99

Fanny Fern

"

When grandparents enter the door, discipline flies out the window.

"

Ogden Nash

66

Grandmother:
A wonderful mother
with lots of practice.

99

Unknown

> 66
>
> Grandma always made you feel she had been waiting to see just you all day and now the day was complete.
>
> 99

Marcy DeMaree

66

If God had intended
us to follow recipes,
He wouldn't have given
us grandmothers.

99

Linda Henley

66

Nobody can do for little children what grandparents do. Grandparents sort of sprinkle stardust over the lives of little children.

99

Alex Haley

❝

Grandmas are moms
with lots of frosting.

❞

Unknown

66

Your grandma is a magician.
Remember that time when you fell
off your bicycle and she lifted you up
onto the kitchen counter? She cleaned
your bloody knees, washed the tears
and snot off your face, told you funny
stories and tickled your stomach
until you giggled so hard it made you
hiccup. The tears, the blood, the pain,
your mum's closed bedroom door – all
vanished as if your grandma had
waved a wand – sim sala bim!

99

Margrét Helgadóttir

66

A faint smell of lilac filled the air. There was always lilac in this part of town. Where there were grandmothers, there was always lilac.

99

Laura Miller

"

A grandmother is a remarkable
woman. She's a wonderful
combination of warmth and
kindness, laughter and love.

"

Unknown

❝

No one ... who has not
known that inestimable
privilege can possibly realize
what good fortune it is to
grow up in a home where
there are grandparents.

❞

Suzanne La Follette

66

If grandmas hadn't existed, kids would have inevitably invented them.

99

Arthur Kornhaber

66

Young people need something
stable to hang on to – a culture
connection, a sense of their own
past, a hope for their own future.
Most of all, they need what
grandparents can give them.

99

Jay Kesler

66

Because [grandparents] are usually free to love and guide and befriend the young without having to take daily responsibility for them, they can often reach out past pride and fear of failure and close the space between generations.

99

Jimmy Carter

66

You do not really understand something unless you can explain it to your grandmother.

99

Albert Einstein

66

Grandma and Grandpa, tell me a story and snuggle me with your love. When I'm in your arms, the world seems small and we're blessed by the heavens above.

99

Laura Spiess

66

When it seems the
world can't understand,
your grandmother's
there to hold your hand.

99

Joyce K. Allen Logan

CHAPTER 2

An Ode to Granny

Every grandmother
has their own unique brand
of magic, so here we let the
grandchildren have their say,
as well as finding out
about some of the OG
(Original Grandmothers)
of history.

66

I am where I am today
because my grandmother
gave me the foundation
for success.

99

Oprah Winfrey

66

You are the sun,
Grandma, you are the
sun in my life.

99

Kitty Tsui

❝

My grandmother is my angel on earth.

❞

Catherine Pulsifer

66

We should all have one person who knows how to bless us despite the evidence. Grandmother was that person to me.

99

Phyllis Theroux

**Famous Grandmothers
of History #1:**

Queen Victoria

1819–1901
Queen of the United Kingdom

Mother to George V, King of the
United Kingdom, Wilhelm II, German
Emperor and King of Prussia, Nicholas II,
Emperor of Russia, King of Congress
Poland and Grand Duke of Finland,
Queen Victoria was known as
the "Grandmother of Europe". Her nine
children produced 42 grandchildren
and 87 great-grandchildren.

66

As I learned from growing up, you don't mess with your grandmother.

99

Prince William

66

We believed in our grandmother's cooking more fervently than we believed in God.

99

Jonathan Safran Foer

66

I feel like my grandparents
and parents gave me a
tremendous amount. And if
I can pass some of that on,
then I'll be very happy.

99

Caroline Kennedy

"

My grandmother was the best. She didn't talk much. She spoke very softly when she did, although she had truly a huge voice; when she sang in church, the windows would rattle.

"

Maya Angelou

"

Grandmother… was the
cornerstone of our family, and
a woman of extraordinary
accomplishment, strength and
humility… Our debt to her is
beyond measure.

"

Barack Obama

**Famous Grandmothers
of History #2:**

Eleanor
of Aquitaine

1122–1204
Queen consort of France, Queen of England
and Duchess of Aquitaine

Arguably the most powerful woman
in 12th-century Europe, thanks to her
impressive family tree, Eleanor was
known as the "Grandmother of Europe"
700 years before Queen Victoria
received the same nickname.

66

My grandmother was an
unparalleled storyteller who
gave me a preview of how life
might turn out, and also
fortified my empathy.

99

Chris Ware

> **"**
> She was my buddy, you know what I'm saying. If you could go to heaven right now and say, 'Where is Estelle Talley?' Do that interview. Because that's who knows me. Nobody else.
> **"**

Jamie Foxx

66

My mother and
grandmother raised me.
Queens raised me.

99

Lamar Odom

66

When she smiles, the lines in her face become epic narratives that trace the stories of generations that no book can replace.

99

Curtis Tyrone Jones

66

I loved their home. Everything smelled older, worn but safe; the food aroma had baked itself into the furniture.

99

Susan Strasberg

**Famous Grandmothers
of History #3:**

Marie Curie

1867–1934
Polish-born French physicist

The first woman to win a
Nobel prize, and the only woman
to win the award in two different
fields, Marie was an inspiration
to many, not least of all her
daughters and grandchildren.

66

I have frequently been
questioned, especially by women,
of how I could reconcile family
life with a scientific career. Well,
it has not been easy.

99

Marie Curie

66

I knew I could count
on her, and I knew
she loved me.

99

Carol Burnett

66

Her crown of white hair seemed to stand like a halo around her in the night sky.

99

Lilian Li

**Famous Grandmothers
of History #4:**

Louisa Adams

1775–1852
First Lady of the United States

As well as being the wife of
John Quincy Adams, the
sixth president of the United States,
and the first foreign-born
First Lady of the United States,
Louisa was mother to four children
and grandmother to around
10 children.

66

I have been grateful for the influence of my grandmother and my grandfather in my life. I remember my grandmother as a queenly woman.

99

James E. Faust

66

My grandmother had a love
which found in me so totally
its complement, its goal, its
constant lodestar, that the genius
of great men, all the genius that
might ever have existed from the
beginning of the world, would
have been less precious to my
grandmother than a single one
of my defects.

99

Marcel Proust

66

When your grandmother
is a whirlwind, you get
spun along whether you
want to or not.

99

Kate Morton

66

My grandmother was a Jewish juggler: she used to worry about six things at once.

99

Richard Lewis

66

I could do worse than become
my own grandma, or anyone of
the strong women who raised
us. Our strengths emerged from
theirs; we build on their heritage
and transform their resilience
and competence into our own.

99

Regina Barreca

**Famous Grandmothers
of History #5:**

Queen Rania

1970–present
Queen of Jordan

Born to Palestinian refugees,
Queen Rania has only just begun her
journey as a maternal grandmother,
and perhaps the most stylish one at
that. Although, it is her work
advocating for children's peace and
education that has allowed her to
act as a mother and grandmother to
children all around the world.

66

We have a saying in Arabic that no person is dearer to us more than our children than our grandchildren.

99

Queen Rania of Jordan

66

Grandmam, as I have seen in
looking back, was the decider
of my fate. She shaped my life,
without of course knowing
what my life would be.
She taught me many things that
I was going to need to know,
without either us knowing
I would need to know them.

99

Wendell Berry

"

Grandma must have come to inspect the settings a hundred times, being a perfectionist. Her love was evident in every little thing that was present in the house. It was soothing to be back in the house.

"

Preethi Venugopala

**Famous Grandmothers
of History #6:**

Catherine de' Medici

1519–1589
Queen Consort and Queen Regent of France

Mother to kings and queens,
Charles IX, Henry III and Margaret and
Elisabeth of Valois, and grandmother to
around 15 children, Catherine played
a significant role in shaping the course
of 16th-century France.

"

She seems to have had the ability to stand firmly on the rock of her past while living completely and unregretfully in the present.

"

Madeleine L'Engle

66

My grandmother is over 80 and still doesn't need glasses. Drinks right out of the bottle.

99

Henry Youngman

66

My grandmother started walking five miles a day when she was 60. She's 97 now, and we don't know where the heck she is.

99

Ellen DeGeneres

66

To all of the grandmothers
who make the world more
gentle, more tolerant and more
safe for our children. Never
doubt your importance.

99

Mary-Lou Rosengren

66

As a child I knew
almost nothing,
nothing beyond what
I had picked up in my
grandmother's house.

99

V. S. Naipaul

Famous Grandmothers of History #7:

Ruth Bader Ginsberg

1933–2020

Associate Justice of the Supreme Court
of the United States

Known for her legal acumen
and fight for gender equality, Ruth
was more than the first Jewish woman
and the second woman to serve
on the Supreme Court, she was also
a loved "Bubbie".

66

The daughter and granddaughter of these immigrants sits on the highest court in the land and will proudly administer the oath of citizenship to you.

99

Ruth Bader Ginsburg

"

My grandmother
was the only
grandmother I ever met
who smoked cigars.

""

Road Dahl
The Witches, 1983

"

Some grandmas took their grandchildren to parks, or bought them books and dolls, or shared their special stories. Her grandma shared her recipes.

"

Amy E. Reichert
The Coincidence of Coconut Cake, 2015

Maria Theresa
of Austria

1717–1780

Holy Roman Empress and Archduchess of Austria

Maria Theresa's legacy and reforms
had long-lasting impacts on Europe, but
most of all, her wish was to have as many
grandchildren as possible. At the time
of her death, she had around two dozen
grandchildren, of which all the eldest
surviving daughters were named after her,
with the exception of just one.

66

It's possible to love
your grandmother for
years and years without
really knowing anything
about her.

99

Fredrik Backman

CHAPTER 3

A Mother's Grand Rebirth

They say that when a baby is born,
so is a grandmother.

And by all accounts, it's an
altogether more joyful role than that
of "mother", one characterized
by uncomplicated adoration
and a total inability to say the
word "no"…

66

Becoming a grandmother turns the page. Line by line you are rewritten. You are tilted off your old centre, spun onto new turf. There's a faint scent of déjà vu from when you raised your own children, but this place feels freer.

99

Lesley Stahl

"

Becoming a grandmother
is wonderful. One
moment you're just a
mother. The next you are
all-wise and prehistoric.

"

Pam Brown

66

Being a mother and grandmother is the best of the best in my life. My grandchildren multiply the joy my daughters bring me.

99

Alexandra Stoddard

66

Grandmotherhood initiated
me into a world of play, where
all things became fresh, alive,
and honest again through my
grandchildren's eyes. Mostly,
it retaught me love.

99

Sue Monk Kidd

"

So, what do I really know
about being a grandmother?
Well, I remember what I didn't
like as a child. I also loved being
a mom, but I have to tell you
that being a grandmother has
brought a whole new side of life
– the fun side – to me.

"

Janet Steele

66

It's such a grand
thing to be a mother
of a mother – that's
why the world calls her
grandmother.

99

Unknown

"

I often can't tell what makes me do things. Sometimes I do them just to find out what I feel like doing them. And sometimes I do them because I want to have some exciting things to tell my grandchildren.

"

Lucy Maud Montgomery

"

Grandchildren are the crown of the aged.

"

Proverbs 17:6

66

Your children are
your rainbows and
your grandchildren are
your pot of gold.

99

Irish blessing

"

The reason
grandchildren and
grandparents get along
so well is that they have
a common enemy.

"

Sam Levenson

"

A mother becomes a true grandmother the day she stops noticing the terrible things her children do because she is so enchanted with the wonderful things her grandchildren do.

"

Lois Wyse

"

Grandchildren are
God's way of
compensating us for
growing old.

"

Mary H. Waldrip

> **66**
>
> For myself, one of the sweetest words I have ever heard is 'Nana'.
>
> **99**

Zelda Rosenbaum

66

Grandchildren make you feel
great about life, and yourself,
and your ability to love someone
unconditionally, finally, after
all these years.

99

Anne Lamott

"

It is as grandmothers that our mothers come into the fullness of their grace.

"

Christopher Morley

"

Grandmother opens
up a new world of
change, challenge,
and celebration in a
woman's life.

"

Rebecca Barlow Jordan

"

Many of my friends were
grandmothers and, without
exception, they said, 'Until you
become a grandmother, you
can't understand how it feels.'

""

Barbara LoMonaco

66

If becoming a
grandmother was only
a matter of choice,
I should advise every
one of you straight away
to become one.

99

Hannah Whithall Smith

"

Perfect love sometimes does not come until the first grandchild.

"

Welsh proverb

66

Being a grandmother provides
you with an opportunity to help
your grandchild gain a sense of
who he or she really is.

99

Deborah Williams and Linda A. Johnson

66

Just about the time a woman thinks her work is done, she becomes a grandmother.

99

Edward H. Dreschnack

"

Truth be told, being a grandma is as close as we ever get to perfection. The ultimate warm sticky bun with plump raisins and nuts. Clouds nine, ten, and eleven.

"

Bryna Nelson Paston

"

If I had known how
wonderful it would be to
have grandchildren,
I'd have had them first.

"

Lois Wyse

66

You make all your mistakes with your own children so by the time your grandchildren arrive, you know how to get it right. Plus, once you turn fifty, you kind of stop caring what others think.

99

Liz Fenton

66

I used to think I was
too old to fall in love
again. Then I became
a grandma.

99

Unknown

"

Being a grandmother
is the best – it can't
be overrated.

"

Marty Norman

A grandmother once said
that children are the
investments and grandchildren
the dividends.

Selma Berg

66

A grandchild is different.
Gone are the bonds of guilt
and responsibility that burden
the maternal relationship.
The way to love is free.

99

Kate Morton

CHAPTER 4

Pearls of Wisdom

As well as being a shoulder to cry on, grandmothers can always be relied on to provide their own special brand of wisdom.

So, now that we're feeling all warm and fuzzy, it's time to take heed of the sage advice only grandma could dispense, and you might learn some trivia that even she might be impressed with along the way…

66

Patience is a virtue.

99

Translation: Stop asking me when
the muffins will be ready.

"

Always save for a
rainy day.

"

Translation: Put some money away for emergencies.

Grandmothers are called by various names around the world, such as "Nana", "Granny", "Grandma", "Mimi", "Abuela", "Nani" and "Oma".

“
Never go to bed angry.
”

Translation: **Resolve arguments before the day finishes.**

Globally, there are over 1 billion grandmothers.

It is thought that 72% of them provide regular care for their grandchildren.

66

Kindness costs nothing but means everything.

99

Translation: Well, this one needs no
explanation, does it?

66

A stitch in time saves nine.

99

Translation: Fix something when you first notice it, before it becomes a bigger problem.

66

Count your blessings.

99

Translation: Be grateful for what you have –
it's likely more than you realize.

World's Youngest
Grandmother

The youngest grandmother on record was Rifca Stanescu from Romania, who became a grandmother at the age of 23 in 2011.

66

The best things in life aren't things.

99

Translation: Money and possessions are
not the answer.

66

Measure twice, cut once.

99

Translation: **Take care, and save yourself
some time in the long run.**

61% of grandparents
provide financial
support or gifts for
their grandchildren.

66

My grandmother would say,
'Make sure you look good.
Make sure you speak well.
Make sure you remain that
Southern gentleman that
I've taught you to be.'

99

Jamie Foxx

66

You catch more
flies with honey than
with vinegar.

99

Translation: You'll achieve more if
you're nice to people.

Longest-Lived
Grandmother

The oldest known woman listed in the Guinness World Records is Jeanne Louise Calment who lived to be 122 years old.

Jeanne had one daughter, who went on to have her own child, making Jeanne the oldest grandmother in modern times.

“

My grandmother
always told me how you
start is how you finish.

”

Bernie Mac

___

66

Laughter is the best medicine.

99

Translation: Stay positive!

___

66

Granny always said
finding justice was as
tough as putting socks
on a rooster.

99

Jessica Maria Tuccelli

66

The pen is mightier than the sword.

99

Translation: Nothing is more powerful than a strongly worded letter...

"

Don't put all your eggs
in one basket.

"

Translation: Diversify, diversify, diversify, or you
could lose everything in one fell swoop.

In some whale species, such as orcas (killer whales), grandmothers play crucial roles in family groups by helping to care for and protect their grandchildren.

"

Hope for the best,
plan for the worst.

99

Translation: **A healthy dose of realism
never hurt anyone.**

66

Save your pennies and the dollars/pounds earn themselves.

99

Translation: **Even small savings make a difference over time.**

66

His grandmother had taught him that
there was no such thing as coincidence.
There are millions of people in this
world, she had told him, and the spirits
will see that most of them, you never
have to meet. But there are one or two
that you are tied to, and spirits will
cross you back and forth, threading so
many knots until they catch and you
finally get it right.

99

Jodi Picoult

"*Grandma*"
Around the World

Spanish: Abuela, Abuelita, Tita, Lita

French: Grand-mère, Mamie, Mémé

Italian: Nonna, Nonnina, Nonnarella

German: Oma, Omi, Großmutter

Dutch: Oma, Grootmoeder,
Bomma (Belgian Dutch)

Portuguese: Avó, Vovó, Avozinha

Polish: Babcia, Babunia

Greek: Γιαγιά *(Yiayia)*

Turkish: *Büyükanne, Nene*

Chinese (Mandarin):
奶奶 *(Nǎinai)*, 外婆 *(Wàipó)*

Japanese: おばあちゃん *(Obāchan)*

Korean: 할머니 *(Halmeoni)*

Arabic: جدة *(Jadda)*

Swedish: Mormor (maternal),
Farmor (paternal)

Norwegian: *Bestemor*

Finnish: Mummo

66

You can't take your money with you.

99

Translation: Don't hoard your wealth –
share it with others.

66

Don't cry over spilled milk.

99

Translation: There's no point ruminating
on things you can't change.

Emma Gatewood,

better known
as "Grandma Gatewood",
became the first woman
to hike the entire
2168 miles (3849 km) of
the Appalachian Trail solo,
in 1955, at the age of 67.

"
Early to bed,
early to rise.

"

Translation: **Prioritize your sleep!**

Many countries have special days to honour grandmothers, such as Grandparents' Day in the United States and various Grandmothers' Days celebrated in countries like Italy, Poland and Spain.

"

Don't sweat the small stuff.

"

Translation: If it's not important, let it go.

66

Don't spend what you don't have.

99

Translation: Put that credit card away...

66

Our grandmother
didn't like the word
retirement, she
said life is for living
not for retiring.

99

Catherine Pulsifer

CHAPTER 5

Head of Silver, Heart of Gold

Let us finish this compendium
by revelling in the unwavering,
unconditional love that
only a grandmother can offer, and
by remembering those women who
have shaped us, loved us and,
in their own special way, made the
world a brighter place.

66

If you're lucky enough to still have grandparents, visit them, cherish them and celebrate them while you can.

99

Regina Brett

"

Grandparents make
the world a little softer,
a little kinder, a little
warmer.

"

Unknown

❝

There is no other love that's as special as the love of a grandma. So warm and fuzzy, so calm and sweet, so cheerful and joyful.

❞

Hopal Green

66

Some moments can
only be cured with a big
squishy grandma hug.

99

Dan Pearce

66

She loved them so much
that she felt a kind of hollowness
on the inner surface of her arms
whenever she looked at
them – an ache of longing to
pull them close and hold them
tight against her.

99

Anne Tyler

"

Surely, two of the most
satisfying experiences
in life must be those of
being a grandchild or
a grandparent.

"

Donald A. Norberg

66

Nobody can replace the love of a grandma. She has this magical ability to make everything feel better.

99

Unknown

66

Grandmas never run out
of hugs or cookies.

99

Unknown

"

They say genes skip generations. Maybe that's why grandparents find their grandchildren so likeable.

"

Joan McIntosh

66

Her grandmother, as she gets older, is not fading but rather becoming more concentrated.

99

Paulette Alden

66

Who needs a fairy godmother when you have a grandma?

99

Unknown

"

No cowboy was ever faster on the draw than a grandmother pulling a baby picture out of a wallet.

"

Unknown

66

Grandchildren never outgrow grandma's arms.

99

Unknown

66

There are grandmothers
out there who would
move heaven and earth
for their grandchildren.

99

Janice Elliott-Howard

66

Sometimes our grandmas and grandpas are like grand-angels.

99

Lexie Saige

66

I know what it is like
to be brought up with
unconditional love.
In my life that came
from my grandmother.

99

André Leon Talley

"

No spring, nor summer
hath such grace.
As I have seen in one
autumnal face.

"

John Donne

66

If you are lucky enough to have
your grandmother with you, sit
and talk with her sometime.
Ask her big questions, like what's
the secret to a happy marriage,
and little ones, like when was
the first time she put on lipstick.

99

Erin Bried

66

Grandmothers are everything
in life: If you need a friend,
Grandma is willing to be your
best friend ever.

99

Euginia Herlihy

66

A garden of love grows
in a grandmother's heart.

99

Unknown

> **66**
>
> If nothing is going well,
> call your grandmother.
>
> **99**

Italian proverb

66

Grandmas don't just say
'that's nice' – they reel back
and roll their eyes and
throw up their hands and smile.
You get your money's worth
out of grandmas.

99

Unknown

66

It's impossible for a grandmother to understand that few people, and maybe none, will find her grandchild as endearing as she does.

99

Janet Lanese

"

Unconditional
positive regard is rarely
given by anyone
except a grandparent.

"

Unknown

66

Grandma has ears that truly listen, arms that always hold, love that's never ending, and a heart that is made of gold.

99

Unknown

"

Having a grandmother is
like having an army. This is a
grandchild's ultimate privilege:
knowing that someone is on
your side, always, whatever
the details. Even when you are
wrong. Especially then, in fact.
A grandmother is both a sword
and a shield.

"

Fredrik Backman

66

I thought grandmothers
had to like you. It's a
law or something.

99

Mary E. Pearson

66

If your baby is 'beautiful and
perfect, never cries or fusses,
sleeps on schedule and burps on
demand, an angel all the time,'
you're the grandma.

99

Teresa Bloomingdale

66

This is a place where grandmothers hold babies on their laps under the stars and whisper in their ears that the lights in the sky are holes in the floor of heaven.

99

Rick Bragg

66

A grandmother thinks of her
grandchildren day and night,
even when they are not with her.
She will always love them more
than anyone would understand.

99

Karen Gibbs

66

Between the earth
and sky above,
nothing can match a
grandmother's love.

99

Unknown

66

Grandmothers are a gift not to
be taken lightly. So many lose
them, before they are old enough
to know their magic.

99

Nikita Gill

66

There's no place
like home,
except Grandma's.

99

Unknown